T0071878

Theodore Roosevelt
on Bravery

Theodore Roosevelt on Bravery

Lessons from the Most Courageous Leader of the Twentieth Century

Skyhorse Publishing

Skyhorse Publishing books may be purchased in bulk at special discounts for sales promotion, corporate gifts, fund-raising, or educational purposes. Special editions can also be created to specifications. For details, contact the Special Sales Department, Skyhorse Publishing, 307 West 36th Street, 11th Floor, New York, NY 10018 or info@skyhorsepublishing.com.

Skyhorse® and Skyhorse Publishing® are registered trademarks of Skyhorse Publishing, Inc.®, a Delaware corporation.

Visit our website at www.skyhorsepublishing.com.

10 9 8 7 6 5 4

Library of Congress Cataloging-in-Publication Data is available on file.

Cover design by Jane Sheppard
Cover photo credit Jane Sheppard

Print ISBN: 978-1-63220-281-9
Ebook ISBN: 978-1-63220-805-7

Printed in the United States of America

"Believe you can and you're halfway there."

"In any moment of decision, the best thing you can do is the right thing, the next best thing is the wrong thing, and the worst thing you can do is nothing."

"If you could kick the person in the pants responsible for most of your trouble, you wouldn't sit for a month."

"With self-discipline most anything is possible."

"Every man among us is more fit to meet the duties and responsibilities of citizenship because of the perils over which, in the past, the nation has triumphed; because of the blood and sweat and tears, the labor and the anguish, through which, in the days that have gone, our forefathers moved on to triumph."

"People ask the difference between a leader and a boss. The leader leads, and the boss drives."

"Great thoughts speak only to the thoughtful mind, but great actions speak to all mankind."

"Nobody cares how much you know, until they know how much you care."

"If we stand idly by, if we seek merely swollen, slothful ease and ignoble peace, if we shrink from the hard contests where men must win at hazard of their lives and at the risk of all they hold dear, then the bolder and stronger peoples will pass us by, and will win for themselves the domination of the world."

"The only man who never makes a mistake is the man who never does anything."

"Old age is like everything else. To make a success of it, you've got to start young."

"Keep your eyes on the stars, and your feet on the ground."

"You often hear people speaking as if life was like striving upward toward a mountain peak. That is not so. Life is as if you were traveling a ridge crest. You have the gulf of inefficiency on one side and the gulf of wickedness on the other, and it helps not to have avoided one gulf if you fall into the other."

"If in this country we ever have to face a state of things in which on one side stand the men of high ideals who are honest, good, well-meaning, pleasant people, utterly unable to put those ideals into shape in the rough field of practical life, while on the other side are grouped the strong, powerful, efficient men with no ideals: then the end of the Republic will be near. The salvation of the Republic depends the salvation of our whole social system depends upon the production year by year of a sufficient number of citizens who possess high ideals combined with the practical power to realize them in actual life."

"If there ever was a pursuit which stultified itself by its very conditions, it is the pursuit of pleasure as the all-sufficing end of life. Happiness can not come to any man capable of enjoying true happiness unless it comes as the sequel to duty well and honestly done. To do that duty you need to have more than one trait."

"I want to speak to you first of all as regards your duties as boys; and in the next place as regards your duties as men; and the two things hang together. The same qualities that make a decent boy make a decent man. They have different manifestations, but fundamentally they are the same. If a boy has not got pluck and honesty and commonsense he is a pretty poor creature; and he is a worse creature if he is a man and lacks any one of those three traits."

"A sound body is good; a sound mind is better; but a strong and clean character is better than either."

"Remember that in life, and above all in the very active, practical, workaday life on this continent, the man who wins out must be the man who works. He can not play all the time. He can not have play as his principal occupation and win out. Let him play; let him have as good a time as he can have. I have a pity that is akin to contempt for the man who does not have as good a time as he can out of life. But let him work. Let him count in the world. When he comes to the end of his life let him feel he has pulled his weight and a little more."

"Of course, the worst of all lives is the vicious life; the life of a man who becomes a positive addition to the forces of evil in a community. Next to that and when I am speaking to people who, by birth and training and standing, ought to amount to a great deal, I have a right to say only second to it in criminality comes the life of mere vapid ease, the ignoble life of a man who desires nothing from his years but that they shall be led with the least effort, the least trouble, the greatest amount of physical enjoyment or intellectual enjoyment of a mere dilettante type. The life that is worth living, and the only life that is worth living, is the life of effort, the life of effort to attain what is worth striving for."

"The ideal that it is impossible for a man to strive after in practical life is not the type of ideal that you wish to hold up and follow. Be practical as well as generous in your ideals. Keep your eyes on the stars, but remember to keep your feet on the ground. Be truthful; a lie implies fear, vanity or malevolence; and be frank; furtiveness and insincerity are faults incompatible with true manliness. Be honest, and remember that honesty counts for nothing unless back of it lie courage and efficiency."

"The only time you really live fully is from thirty to sixty. The young are slaves to dreams; the old servants of regrets. Only the middle-aged have all their five senses in the keeping of their wits."

"It is hard to fail, but it is worse never to have tried to succeed."

"The boy who is going to make a great man must not make up his mind merely to overcome a thousand obstacles, but to win in spite of a thousand repulses and defeats."

"The most important single ingredient in the formula of success is knowing how to get along with people."

"When you are asked if you can do a job, tell 'em, 'Certainly I can!' Then get busy and find out how to do it."

"We are face-to-face with our destiny and we must meet it with a high and resolute courage."

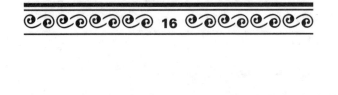

"Greatness means strife for nation and man alike. A soft, easy life is not worth living, if it impairs the fibre of brain and heart and muscle. We must dare to be great; and we must realize that greatness is the fruit of toil and sacrifice and high courage."

"Do what you can, with what you have, where you are."

"The worst lesson that can be taught a man is to rely upon others and to whine over his sufferings."

"I don't pity any man who does hard work worth doing. I admire him. I pity the creature who does not work, at whichever end of the social scale he may regard himself as being."

"I cannot consent to take the position that the door of hope—the door of opportunity—is to be shut upon any man, no matter how worthy, purely upon the grounds of race or color. Such an attitude would, according to my convictions, be fundamentally wrong."

"I am only an average man, but by George, I work harder at it than the average man."

"Gentlemen: you have now reached the last point. If anyone of you doesn't mean business let him say so now. An hour from now will be too late to back out. Once in, you've got to see it through. You've got to perform without flinching whatever duty is assigned you, regardless of the difficulty or the danger attending it. If it is garrison duty, you must attend to it. If it is meeting fever, you must be willing. If it is the closest kind of fighting, anxious for it. You must know how to ride, how to shoot, how to live in the open. Absolute obedience to every command is your first lesson. No matter what comes you mustn't squeal. Think it over—all of you. If any man wishes to withdraw he will be gladly excused, for others are ready to take his place."

"There were all kinds of things I was afraid of at first, ranging from grizzly bears to 'mean' horses and gun-fighters; but by acting as if I was not afraid I gradually ceased to be afraid."

"Courage is not having the strength to go on; it is going on when you don't have the strength."

"I have never in my life envied a human being who led an easy life; I have envied a great many people who led difficult lives and led them well."

"We cannot avoid meeting great issues. All that we can determine for ourselves is whether we shall meet them well or ill."

"There are good men and bad men of all nationalities, creeds and colors; and if this world of ours is ever to become what we hope some day it may become, it must be by the general recognition that the man's heart and soul, the man's worth and actions, determine his standing."

"Above all, let us shrink from no strife, moral or physical, within or without the nation, provided we are certain that the strife is justified, for it is only through strife, through hard and dangerous endeavor, that we shall ultimately win the goal of true national greatness."

"To any nation that stands for human liberties, they have an ally in the United States."

"The good citizen is the man who, whatever his wealth or his poverty, strives manfully to do his duty to himself, to his family, to his neighbor, to the States; who is incapable of the baseness which manifests itself either in arrogance or in envy, but who while demanding justice for himself is no less scrupulous to do justice to others."

"This country will not be a permanently good place for any of us to live in unless we make it a reasonably good place for all of us to live in."

"There are plenty of decent legislators, and plenty of able legislators; but the blamelessness and the fighting edge are not always combined. Both qualities are necessary for the man who is to wage active battle against the powers that prey. He must be clean of life, so that he can laugh when his public or his private record is searched; and yet being clean of life will not avail him if he is either foolish or timid. He must walk warily and fearlessly, and while he should never brawl if he can avoid it, he must be ready to hit hard if the need arises. Let him remember, by the way, that the unforgivable crime is soft hitting. Do not hit at all if it can be avoided; but *never* hit softly."

"If I must choose between righteousness and peace, I choose righteousness."

"If a man does not have an ideal and try to live up to it, then he becomes a mean, base, and sordid creature, no matter how successful."

"No nation deserves to exist if it permits itself to lose the stern and virile virtues; and this without regard to whether the loss is due to the growth of a heartless and all-absorbing commercialism, to prolonged indulgence in luxury and soft, effortless ease, or to the deification of a warped and twisted sentimentality."

"We must ever bear in mind that the great end in view is righteousness, justice as between man and man, nation and nation, the chance to lead our lives on a somewhat higher level, with a broader spirit of brotherly goodwill one for another. Peace is generally good in itself, but it is never the highest good unless it comes as the handmaid of righteousness; and it becomes a very evil thing if it serves merely as a mask for cowardice and sloth, or as an instrument to further the ends of despotism or anarchy."

"Our country—this great republic—means nothing unless it means the triumph of a real democracy, the triumph of popular government, and, in the long run, of an economic system under which each man shall be guaranteed the opportunity to show the best that there is in him."

"A broken promise is bad enough in private life. It is worse in the field of politics. No man is worth his salt in public life who makes on the stump a pledge which he does not keep after election; and, if he makes such a pledge and does not keep it, hunt him out of public life."

"We cannot afford weakly to blind ourselves to the actual conflict which faces us today. The issue is joined, and we must fight or fail."

"I should be heartily ashamed of any American who did not try to make the American government act as justly toward the other nations in international relations as he himself would act toward any individual in private relations. I should be heartily ashamed to see us wrong a weaker power, and I should hang my head forever if we tamely suffered wrong from a stronger power."

"We must have the right kind of character—character that makes a man, first of all, a good man in the home, a good father, and a good husband—that makes a man a good neighbor. You must have that, and, then, in addition, you must have the kind of law and the kind of administration of the law which will give to those qualities in the private citizen the best possible chance for development. The prime problem of our nation is to get the right type of good citizenship, and, to get it, we must have progress, and our public men must be genuinely progressive."

"Great thoughts speak only to the thoughtful mind, but great actions speak to all mankind."

"I care not what others think of what I do, but I care very much about what I think of what I do! That is character!"

"Get action. Seize the moment. Man was never intended to become an oyster."

"It is only through strife, labor, and painful effort, by grim energy and resolute courage, that we move on to better things."

"We can have no '50-50' allegiance in this country. Either a man is an American and nothing else, or he is not an American at all."

"Courtesy is as much a mark of a gentleman as courage."

"Toward all other nations, large and small, our attitude must be one of cordial and sincere friendship. We must show not only in our words, but in our deeds, that we are earnestly desirous of securing their good will by acting toward them in a spirit of just and generous recognition of all their rights. But justice and generosity in a nation, as in an individual, count most when shown not by the weak but by the strong."

"While ever careful to refrain from wrongdoing others, we must be no less insistent that we are not wronged ourselves. We wish peace, but we wish the peace of justice, the peace of righteousness. We wish it because we think it is right and not because we are afraid. No weak nation that acts manfully and justly should ever have cause to fear us, and no strong power should ever be able to single us out as a subject for insolent aggression."

"We know that self-government is diffi-cult. We know that no people needs such high traits of character as that people which seeks to govern its affairs aright through the freely expressed will of the freemen who compose it. But we have faith that we shall not prove false to the memories of the men of the mighty past. They did their work, they left us the splendid heritage we now enjoy. We in our turn have an assured confi-dence that we shall be able to leave this heri-tage unwasted and enlarged to our children and our children's children."

"Much has been given us, and much will rightfully be expected from us. We have duties to others and duties to ourselves; and we can shirk neither. We have become a great nation, forced by the fact of its greatness into relations with the other nations of the earth, and we must behave as beseems a people with such responsibilities."

"It is true of the Nation, as of the individual, that the greatest doer must also be a great dreamer."

"Power invariably means both responsibility and danger."

". . . we must show, not merely in great crises, but in the everyday affairs of life, the qualities of practical intelligence, of courage, of hardihood, and endurance, and above all the power of devotion to a lofty ideal, which made great the men who founded this Republic in the days of Washington, which made great the men who preserved this Republic in the days of Abraham Lincoln."

"Probably the greatest harm done by vast wealth is the harm that we of moderate means do ourselves when we let the vices of envy and hatred enter deep into our own natures."

"Rhetoric is a poor substitute for action, and we have trusted only to rhetoric. If we are really to be a great nation, we must not merely talk; we must act big."

"There has never yet been a man in our history who led a life of ease whose name is worth remembering."

"I think there is only one quality worse than hardness of heart and that is softness of head."

"We should keep steadily before our minds the fact that Americanism is a question of principle, of purpose, of idealism, of character; that it is not a matter of birthplace, or creed, or line of descent."

"The most successful politician is he who says what the people are thinking most often in the loudest voice."

"It behooves every man to remember that the work of the critic is of altogether secondary importance, and that, in the end, progress is accomplished by the man who does things."

"Don't hit at all if it is honorably possible to avoid hitting; but never hit soft."

"Wars are, of course, as a rule to be avoided; but they are far better than certain kinds of peace."

"If there is not the war, you don't get the great general; if there is not a great occasion, you don't get a great statesman; if Lincoln had lived in a time of peace, no one would have known his name."

"When you're at the end of your rope, tie a knot and hold on."

"The men with the muck-rake are often indispensable to the well-being of society, but only if they know when to stop raking the muck."

"I am an American; free born and free bred, where I acknowledge no man as my superior, except for his own worth, or as my inferior, except for his own demerit."

"Knowing what's right doesn't mean much unless you do what's right."

"Here is your country. Cherish these natural wonders, cherish the natural resources, cherish the history and romance as a sacred heritage, for your children and your children's children. Do not let selfish men or greedy interests skin your country of its beauty, its riches or its romance."

"A vote is like a rifle: its usefulness depends upon the character of the user."

"Patriotism means to stand by the country. It does not mean to stand by the president or any other public official, save exactly to the degree in which he himself stands by the country. It is patriotic to support him insofar as he efficiently serves the country. It is unpatriotic not to oppose him to the exact extent that by inefficiency or otherwise he fails in his duty to stand by the country. In either event, it is unpatriotic not to tell the truth, whether about the president or anyone else."

"We despise and abhor the bully, the brawler, the oppressor, whether in private or public life, but we despise no less the coward and the voluptuary. No man is worth calling a man who will not fight rather than submit to infamy or see those that are dear to him suffer wrong."

"There is not a man of us who does not at times need a helping hand to be stretched out to him, and then shame upon him who will not stretch out the helping hand to his brother."

"It is not often that a man can make opportunities for himself. But he can put himself in such shape that when or if the opportunities come he is ready."

"Only those are fit to live who do not fear to die; and none are fit to die who have shrunk from the joy of life and the duty of life."

"Character, in the long run, is the decisive factor in the life of an individual and of nations alike."

"In life, as in football, the principle to follow is to hit the line hard."

"For those who fight for it, life has a flavor the sheltered will never know."

"Far better is it to dare mighty things, to win glorious triumphs, even though checkered by failure . . . than to take rank with those poor spirits who neither enjoy nor suffer much, because they live in a gray twilight that knows not victory nor defeat."

"I wish to preach, not the doctrine of ignoble ease, but the doctrine of the strenuous life, the life of toil and effort, of labor and strife; to preach that highest form of success which comes, not to the man who desires mere easy peace, but to the man who does not shrink from danger, from hardship, or from bitter toil, and who out of these wins the splendid ultimate triumph."

"No man is justified in doing evil on the ground of expediency."

"I put myself in the way of things happening, and they happened."

"The nation behaves well if it treats the natural resources as assets which it must turn over to the next generation increased; and not impaired in value."

"No man is above the law and no man is below it: nor do we ask any man's permission when we ask him to obey it."

"All for each, and each for all, is a good motto; but only on condition that each works with might and main to so maintain himself as not to be a burden to others."

"The worst of all fears is the fear of living."

"At the outset almost every man is frightened when he goes into action, but that the course to follow is for the man to keep such a grip on himself that he can act just as if he was not frightened. After this is kept up long enough it changes from pretense to reality, and the man does in very fact become fearless by sheer dint of practicing fearlessness when he does not feel it."

"Love of peace is common among weak, short-sighted, timid, and lazy persons; and on the other hand courage is found among many men of evil temper and bad character. Neither quality shall by itself avail. Justice among the nations of mankind, and the uplifting of humanity, can be brought about only by those strong and daring men who with wisdom love peace, but who love righteousness more than peace."

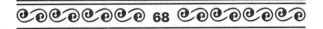

"Americans learn only from catastrophes and not from experience."

"I am a strong individualist by personal habit, inheritance, and conviction; but it is a mere matter of common sense to recognize that the State, the community, the citizens acting together, can do a number of things better than if they were left to individual action."

"For us is the life of action, of strenuous performance of duty; let us live in the harness, striving mightily; let us rather run the risk of wearing out than rusting out."

"The first requisite of a good citizen in this republic of ours is that he shall be able and willing to pull his own weight."

"It is not the critic who counts; not the man who points out how the strong man stumbled or where the doer of deeds could have done them better. The credit belongs to the man who is actually in the arena, whose face is marred by dust and sweat and blood; who strives valiantly; who errs and comes short again and again; who knows great enthusiasms, the great devotions; who spends himself in a worthy cause; who at the best, knows in the end the triumph of high achievement, and who, at the worst, if he fails, at least fails while daring greatly so that his place shall never be with those timid souls who neither know victory nor defeat."

"It was a pleasure to deal with a man of high ideals, who scorned everything mean and base, and who possessed those robust and hardy qualities of body and mind, for the lack of which no merely negative virtue can ever atone."

"Each one must do his part if we wish to show that the nation is worthy of its good fortune."

"A great democracy has got to be progressive or it will soon cease to be great or a democracy."

"Justice consists not in being neutral between right and wrong, but finding out the right and upholding it, wherever found, against the wrong."

"Let the watchwords of all our people be the old familiar watchwords of honesty, decency, fair-dealing, and commonsense."

"In foreign affairs we must make up our minds that, whether we wish it or not, we are a great people and must play a great part in the world. It is not open to us to choose whether we will play that great part or not. We have to play it. All we can decide is whether we shall play it well or ill."

"There is not one among us in whom a devil does not dwell; at some time, on some point, that devil masters each of us . . . It is not having been in the Dark House, but having left it, that counts."

"And it is through strife and the readiness for strife that a man or a nation must win greatness. So, let the world know that we are here and willing to pour out our blood, our treasure, our tears. And that America is ready and if need be desirous of battle."

"No ability, no strength and force, no power of intellect or power of wealth, shall avail us, if we have not the root of right living in us."

"I would rather go out of politics having the feeling that I had done what was right than stay in with the approval of all men, knowing in my heart that I have acted as I ought not to."

"The leader for the time being, whoever he may be, is but an instrument, to be used until broken and then to be cast aside; and if he is worth his salt he will care no more when he is broken than a soldier cares when he is sent where his life is forfeit in order that the victory may be won."

"We Americans have many grave problems to solve, many threatening evils to fight, and many deeds to do, if, as we hope and believe, we have the wisdom, the strength, and the courage and the virtue to do them. But we must face facts as they are. We must neither surrender ourselves to a foolish optimism, nor succumb to a timid and ignoble pessimism."

"The joy of living is his who has the heart to demand it."

". . . if in exceptional cases there is any conflict between the rights of property and the rights of man, then we must stand for the rights of man."

"Dreams are a dime a dozen. It's their execution that counts."

"Nothing worth having was ever achieved without effort."

". . . of this we can be certain, that we shall not go down in ruin unless we deserve and earn our end. There is no necessity for us to fall; we can hew out our destiny for ourselves, if only we have the wit and the courage and the honesty."

"Unjust war is to be abhorred; but woe to the nation that does not make ready to hold its own in time of need against all who would harm it! And woe thrice over to the nation in which the average man loses the fighting edge, loses the power to serve as a soldier if the day of need should arise!"

"I'm as strong as a bull moose and you can use me to the limit."

"Personally, I do not believe that our civilization will fall. I think that on the whole we have grown better and not worse. I think that on the whole the future holds more for us than even the great past has held. But, assuredly, the dreams of golden glory in the future will not come true unless, high of heart and strong of hand, by our own mighty deeds we make them come true. We can not afford to develop any one set of qualities, any one set of activities, at the cost of seeing others, equally necessary, atrophied."

"Americanism means the virtues of courage, honor, justice, truth, sincerity, and hardihood—the virtues that made America. The things that will destroy America are prosperity-at-any-price, peace-at-any-price, safety-first instead of duty-first, the love of soft living and the get-rich-quick theory of life."

"At times a man must cut loose from his associates and stand alone for a great cause; but the necessity for such action is almost as rare as the necessity for revolution."

"Credit should go with the performance of duty, and not with what is very often the accident of glory."

"There can be no life without change, and to be afraid of what is different or unfamiliar is to be afraid of life."

"We must beware of any attempt to make hatred in any form the basis of action. Most emphatically each of us needs to stand up for his own rights; all men and all groups of men are bound to retain their self-respect, and, demanding this same respect from others, to see that they are not injured and that they have secured to them the fullest liberty of thought and action. But to feed fat a grudge against others, while it may or may not harm them, is sure in the long run to do infinitely greater harm to the man himself."

"Peace is normally a great good, and normally it coincides with righteousness, but it is righteousness and not peace which should bind the conscience of a nation as it should bind the conscience of an individual; and neither a nation nor an individual can surrender conscience to another's keeping."

"I had always felt that if there were a serious war I wished to be in a position to explain to my children why I did take part in it, and not why I did not take part in it."

"No man in public position can, under penalty of forfeiting the right to the respect of those whose regard he most values, fail as the opportunity comes to do all that in him lies for peace."

"I have only a second rate brain, but I think I have a capacity for action."

"In advocating any measure we must consider not only its justice but its practicability."

"Bodily vigor is good, and vigor of intellect is even better, but far above both is character. It is true, of course, that a genius may, on certain lines, do more than a brave and manly fellow who is not a genius; and so, in sports, vast physical strength may overcome weakness, even though the puny body may have in it the heart of a lion. But, in the long run, in the great battle of life, no brilliancy of intellect, no perfection of bodily development, will count when weighed in the balance against that assemblage of virtues, active and passive, of moral qualities, which we group together under the name of character; and if between any two contestants, even in college sport or in college work, the difference in character on the right side is as great as the difference of intellect or strength the other way, it is the character side that will win."

"Any man who has met with success, if he will be frank with himself, must admit that there has been a big element of fortune in the success."

"Courage isn't the absence of fear, it's the choice that something else is greater than that fear."

"A man can of course hold public office, and many a man does hold public office, and lead a public career of a sort, even if there are other men who possess secrets about him which he cannot afford to have divulged. But no man can lead a public career really worth leading, no man can act with rugged independence in serious crises, nor strike at great abuses, nor afford to make powerful and unscrupulous foes, if he is himself vulnerable in his private character."

"The most practical kind of politics is the politics of Decency."

"The fundamental thing to do for every man is to give him a chance to reach a place in which he will make the greatest possible contribution to the public welfare. Understand what I say there. Give him a chance, not push him up if he will not be pushed. Help any man who stumbles; if he lies down, it is a poor job to try to carry him; but if he is a worthy man, try your best to see that he gets a chance to show the worth that is in him."

"The only way to get good service is to give somebody power to render it, facing the fact that power which will enable a man to do a job well will also necessarily enable him to do it ill if he is the wrong kind of man."

"Aggressive fighting for the right is the greatest sport in the world."

"No, I'm not a good shot, but I shoot often."

"The United States does not have a choice as to whether or not it will or will not play a great part in the world. Fate has made that choice for us. The only question is whether we will play the part well or badly."

"When you play, play hard; when you work, don't play at all."

"Justice consists not in being neutral between right and wrong, but in finding out the right and upholding it, wherever found, against the wrong."

"The best executive is the one who has sense enough to pick good men to do what he wants done, and self-restraint enough to keep from meddling with them while they do it."

"The most important single ingredient in the formula of success is knowing how to get along with people."

"It is better to be faithful than famous."

"At sometime in our lives a devil dwells within us, causes heartbreaks, confusion and troubles, then dies."

"Obedience of the law is demanded; not asked as a favor."

"The men and women who have the right ideals . . . are those who have the courage to strive for the happiness which comes only with labor and effort and self-sacrifice, and those whose joy in life springs in part from power of work and sense of duty."

"Some men can live up to their loftiest ideals without ever going higher than a basement."

"All the resources we need are in the mind."

"Our chief usefulness to humanity rests on our combining power with high purpose. Power undirected by high purpose spells calamity, and high purpose by itself is utterly useless if the power to put it into effect is lacking."

"The old parties are husks, with no real soul within either, divided on artificial lines, boss-ridden and privilege-controlled, each a jumble of incongruous elements, and neither daring to speak out wisely and fearlessly on what should be said on the vital issues of the day."

"No man is worth his salt who is not ready at all times to risk his well-being, to risk his body, to risk his life, in a great cause."

"Let us speak courteously, deal fairly, and keep ourselves armed and ready."

"Don't foul, don't flinch. Hit the line hard."

"The pacifist is as surely a traitor to his country and to humanity as is the most brutal wrongdoer."

"No people is wholly civilized where a distinction is drawn between stealing an office and stealing a purse."

"The first essential of civilization is law. Anarchy is simply the handmaiden and fore-runner of tyranny and despotism. Law and order enforced with justice and by strength lie at the foundations of civilization."

"While the nation that has dared to be great, that has had the will and the power to change the destiny of the ages, in the end must die, yet no less surely the nation that has played the part of the weakling must also die; and whereas the nation that has done nothing leaves nothing behind it, the nation that has done a great work really continues, though in changed form, to live forever-more."

"Law must be based upon justice, else it cannot stand, and it must be enforced with resolute firmness, because weakness in enforcing it means in the end that there is no justice and no law, nothing but the rule of disorderly and unscrupulous strength."

"We must ever keep the core of our national being sound, and see to it that not only our citizens in private life, but, above all, our statesmen in public life, practice the old commonplace virtues which from time immemorial have lain at the root of all true national wellbeing."

"We have but little room among our people for the timid, the irresolute, and the idle; and it is no less true that there is scant room in the world at large for the nation with mighty thews that dares not to be great."

"You, the sons of the pioneers, if you are true to your ancestry, must make your lives as worthy as they made theirs. They sought for true success, and therefore they did not seek ease. They knew that success comes only to those who lead the life of endeavor."

"It seems to me that the simple acceptance of this fundamental fact of American life, this acknowledgment that the law of work is the fundamental law of our being, will help us to start aright in facing not a few of the problems that confront us from without and from within. As regards internal affairs, it should teach us the prime need of remembering that, after all has been said and done, the chief factor in any man's success or failure must be his own character—that is, the sum of his common sense, his courage, his virile energy and capacity. Nothing can take the place of this individual factor."

"The man who works, the man who does great deeds, in the end dies as surely as the veriest idler who cumbers the earth's surface; but he leaves behind him the great fact that he has done his work well. So it is with nations."

"We admit with all sincerity that our first duty is within our own household; that we must not merely talk, but act, in favor of cleanliness and decency and righteousness, in all political, social, and civic matters. No prosperity and no glory can save a nation that is rotten at heart."

"Let us make it evident that we intend to do justice. Then let us make it equally evident that we will not tolerate injustice being done to us in return. Let us further make it evident that we use no words which we are not prepared to back up with deeds, and that while our speech is always moderate, we are ready and willing to make it good. Such an attitude will be the surest possible guarantee of that self-respecting peace, the attainment of which is and must ever be the prime aim of a self-governing people."

"We shall make mistakes; and if we let these mistakes frighten us from our work we shall show ourselves weaklings."

"[Our country's pioneers] have shown the qualities of daring, endurance, and far-sightedness, of eager desire for victory and stubborn refusal to accept defeat, which go to make up the essential manliness of the American character. Above all, they have recognized in practical form the fundamental law of success in American life—the law of worthy work, the law of high, resolute endeavor."

"Every father and mother here, if they are wise, will bring up their children not to shirk difficulties, but to meet them and overcome them; not to strive after a life of ignoble ease, but to strive to do their duty, first to themselves and their families, and then to the whole state; and this duty must inevitably take the shape of work in some form or other."

"It is impossible to win the great prizes of life without running risks, and the greatest of all prizes are those connected with the home."

"I want to see you shoot the way you shout."

"We must remember not to judge any public servant by any one act, and especially should we beware of attacking the men who are merely the occasions and not the cause of disaster."

"Get action. Seize the moment. Man was never intended to become an oyster."

"Nine-tenths of wisdom consists in being wise in time."

"We need the iron qualities that go with true manhood. We need the positive virtues of resolution, of courage, of indomitable will, of power to do without shrinking the rough work that must always be done."

"Character is far more important than intellect in making a man a good citizen or successful at his calling—meaning by character not only such qualities as honesty and truthfulness, but courage, perseverance and self-reliance."

"The man who loves other countries as much as his own stands on a level with the man who loves other women as much as he loves his own wife."

"The great virtue of my radicalism lies in the fact that I am perfectly ready, if necessary, to be radical on the conservative side."

"A just war is in the long run far better for a nation's soul than the most prosperous peace obtained by acquiescence in wrong or injustice."

"If an American is to amount to anything he must rely upon himself, and not upon the State; he must take pride in his own work, instead of sitting idle to envy the luck of others. He must face life with resolute courage, win victory if he can, and accept defeat if he must, without seeking to place on his fellow man a responsibility which is not theirs."

"Laws are enacted for the benefit of the whole people, and must not be construed as permitting discrimination against some of the people."

"A man's usefulness depends upon his living up to his ideals insofar as he can."

"All daring and courage, all iron endurance of misfortune make for a finer, nobler type of manhood."

"Both life and death are parts of the same Great Adventure."

"I want to see you game, boys, I want to see you brave and manly, and I also want to see you gentle and tender."

"Far and away the best prize that life has to offer is the chance to work hard at work worth doing."

"From the greatest to the smallest, happiness and usefulness are largely found in the same soul, and the joy of life is won in its deepest and truest sense only by those who have not shirked life's burdens."

"A man who is good enough to shed his blood for his country is good enough to be given a square deal afterwards. More than that no man is entitled to, and less than that no man shall have."

"Courage, hard work, self-mastery, and intelligent effort are all essential to successful life."

"Ours is a government of liberty by, through, and under the law."

"In popular government results worth while can only be achieved by men who combine worthy ideals with practical good sense."

". . . Let us therefore boldly face the life of strife, resolute to do our duty well and manfully; resolute to uphold righteousness by deed and by word; resolute to be both honest and brave, to serve high ideals, yet to use practical methods."

"Without the habit of orderly obedience to the law, without the stern enforcement of the laws at the expense of those who defiantly resist them, there can be no possible progress, moral or material, in civilization. There can be no weakening of the law-abiding spirit here at home, if we are permanently to succeed; and just as little can we afford to show weakness abroad."